ROCK STARS

RAY BONDS

CHARTWELL
BOOKS, INC.

This edition published by

CHARTWELL BOOKS, INC.
A Division of
BOOK SALES, INC.
114 Northfield Avenue
Edison, New Jersey 08837

ISBN 0-7858-2155-4
ISBN 978-0-785821-55-7

© 2006 by Compendium Publishing Ltd., 43 Frith Street, London
W1D 4SA, United Kingdom

Cataloging-in-Publication data is available from the Library of Congress

Designer Ian Hughes

Printed in China by Constant Printing Ltd.

Acknowledgments
All images were supplied by EMPICS in the UK. EMPICS are also the
suppliers of Associated Press images to UK picture buyers and these have
been syndicated via EMPICS for this title (and are so credited at the end
of each relevant caption). For more information see www.empics.com.

INTRODUCTION

Featured here are a couple of hundred stars of "rock" out of the literally thousands of individuals or groups/bands that could have been included. To present some and leave out others in a book like this is always going to be subjective: you could provide logical and persuasive arguments for a host of performers who could have been included, and equally for many that have been and, in your opinion, should not. Because of the nature of the subject everyone—depending on age, sex, musical preferences—would have a different view, so these are arguments that could not be won by anybody.

Just take look at the subject itself. From a period stretching back more than fifty changing years, toss into the pot some of the diverse music styles that have made up the miscellany of what we call "rock music" and you will see how impossible it would be for even just two people to agree on which "rock stars" should be in or out: rock 'n' roll, blues, blues-rock, folk-rock, hard rock, glam rock, jazz-rock, classic rock, AOR (Adult Oriented Rock), soul, metal, heavy metal, funk, funk-rock, country-blues, punk, new wave, grunge, pop, dance-pop, disco, Britpop, reggae, ska, hip hop, rap, gangsta-rap, R&B, beat, and so on. Then stir in some "progressives" and "alternatives," plus a pinch of MOR (Middle of the Road)….

Consider next the "stars," those who've been around for decades and who are still earning fortunes from new albums and singles, or performing live to hundreds of thousands of fans, many of whom are of the same pensionable age as the rockers themselves, compared to the one-hit wonders, and those who died young through tragic accidents or illness, or

over-indulgence in things that were not good for them.

Funnily enough, we've included representatives of all of these—music styles and stars—in this book. We've included those rock stars we like and those we don't, those whose music will still be remembered in another fifty years, those who are "in" now but won't be soon, and those who aren't yet but will probably break through any day now.

Whatever your preferences, we are sure you will enjoy our A-Z of boy bands and girl bands, fabulously talented instrumentalists and singers, average but successful strummers and screamers, musicians with a message, and sheer joyful and entertaining performers.

Elvis Presley in 1956: not quite The King yet, but his impact and influence on rock and pop music worldwide were to be enormous. (AP Photo via EMPICS)

Energetic, experimental, fantastically popular worldwide, and hugely profitable, The Beatles were *the* icons of the 1960s, and opened the floodgates for the "British invasion" to the U.S. Here they're seen at a recording session in London, June 1967.

Abba

The Swedish pop group Abba perform the winning 1974 Eurovision Song Contest entry "Waterloo," sung by the girls, Anni-Frid Lyngstad-Fredriksson (Frida), second left, and Agnetha Fältskog (Anna). The other group members, Benny Andersson, left, and Bjorn Ulvaeus, composed the song. The group drifted apart into solo ventures in the early '80s and efforts to persuade them to reform have failed despite reports of multi-million-dollar offers.

AC/DC

Australian heavy-metal band AC/DC's lead singer Brian Johnson (right) and guitarist Angus Young perform in concert at the Carling Hammersmith Apollo in West London, October 21, 2003. The band formed in 1974, becoming instrumental in breaking prejudice against Australian rock. ⇨

Bryan Adams

Canadian Bryan Adams in concert in Zurich, Switzerland, September 16, 2005. Born in 1959, Adams started out at sixteen working with club groups around Vancouver, British Columbia, before hitting the limelight in the early 1980s.

Aerosmith

Steven Tyler, lead singer of the band Aerosmith, performs at the Corel Center in Ottawa, Canada, November, 16, 2005. The band formed at Sunappee, New Hampshire, in 1970.

Anastacia

Apart from of her 2000 smash hit single "I'm Outta Love," New York-born dancer-turned-pop-singer Anastacia has had more success in Europe and Asia than in the U.S. Here she performs during a concert tour through Germany in July 2005.

The Animals

Seen in 1966 with an autograph hunter, members of the British R&B group The Animals hit it big in the '60s with songs such as "The House of The Rising Sun," "We Gotta Get Out of This Place," and "Don't Let Me Be Misunderstood." The group split in 1968, reformed with most of the original line-up in 1977, split again then reformed once more in 1983 for a U.S tour, but split again for good shortly after.

B-52s

Members of the B-52s posing in New York, May 12, 1998, as the musical misfits-turned-pop icons embarked on their first U.S. tour together in nearly a decade. Clockwise from top; Fred Schneider, Keith Strickland, Kate Pierson, and Cindy Wilson. The band formed in Athens, Georgia, in 1976.

Backstreet Boys

The five-member American boy band Backstreet Boys at the 1997 MTV awards in Rotterdam, Netherlands, in November 1997. The band has gone on to be the highest selling boy band, with more than 38 million albums sold in the U.S. alone.

The Beach Boys

Early sixties surfing-scene-inspired group, The Beach Boys are shown in 1966. The group includes three brothers, a cousin, and an honorary relative. Left to right top: Mike Love, Brian Wilson, and Carl Wilson. Bottom: Al Jardine and Dennis Wilson. Driving force behind the band was always Brian Wilson, who is still recording and performing.

The Beastie Boys

The Beastie Boys, from left, Adam Horowitz (also known as Ad-Rock), Mike Diamond (also known as Mike D), and Adam Yauch (also known as MCA), photographed during the Sundance Film Festival in Park City, Utah, January 21, 2006. The Beastie Boys' documentary film, "Awesome: I Fuckin' Shot That," was screened at the Festival. The odd band was formed in Greenwich Village, NYC, in 1981.

The Beatles

The Beatles perform on the CBS "Ed Sullivan Show" in New York, February 9, 1964. At one point during that year they held positions 1, 2, 3, 4, and 5 in the U.S. singles chart, and had seven other singles in the Top 100, while two of their albums were at No. 1 and No. 2. Phenomenal and unbeatable. Final year for the group's activities came in 1969.

The Bee Gees

Tens of thousands of Bee Gees fans packed into London's Wembley Stadium and got down to some real Saturday Night Fever on September 6, 1998, as the veteran British-born but Australia-formed group celebrated three decades at the top of the charts during a world tour. From left to right, Maurice (who died January 12, 2003), Robin, and Barry Gibb. Always ready and able to change with musical fashion, the group is credited with inventing the disco boom.

Pat Benatar

Opera-trained, hard-edged rock vocalist Pat Benatar performs with guitarist and vocalist Neil Giraldo at the South Shore Music Circus in Cohasset, Mass., July 22, 2004. Benatar was born Patricia Andrzejewski in Brooklyn, NYC, January 1953.

⟶

Beyoncé

Powerful-voiced R&B singer/songwriter, actress, record producer, designer, and multi-Grammy Award winner (five in 2004), Beyoncé Knowles (although she performs under her Christian name only) performs during the Destiny Fulfilled Tour at The Pond of Anaheim in Anaheim, California, on September 1, 2005. Shortly after, the Destiny's Child trio (at one time a quartet) released their final album containing their No. 1 hits, and then disbanded, permitting Beyoncé (born in Houston, Texas, September 1981) to carry out filming engagements and to write songs for future solo albums.

Chuck Berry

At seventy-nine years of age, rock 'n' roll legend Chuck Berry performs in the Kongresshaus in Zurich, Switzerland, November 7, 2005. Born in 1926, Berry is regarded by many as the most influential guitarist and songwriter of the entire rock genre, and certainly left his mark with The Beatles and The Rolling Stones, who covered his early material in their performances during the sixties.

Björk

Icelandic pop singer Björk performing at the London Coliseum, in London, September 23, 2001. Classically trained pianist Björk was influenced by punk-rock early in her career. She became lead singer in The Sugarcubes, which disbanded in 1992, with the howlin' and shriekin' Björk embracing a successful singing, songwriting and filming solo career. Born in November 1965, she generally goes by her Christian name only, an Icelandic custom, her surname being Guðmundsdóttir.

The Black Crowes

Vocalist Chris Robinson of The Black Crowes performs with the mixed-genre (hard rock, R&B, blues, country) band in June 2005. The band was formed in Atlanta, Georgia, in 1984, as Mr Crowe's Garden, changing its name to The Black Crowes four years later, and disbanded after the release of the album "Live" in 2002.

Black Sabbath

Ozzy Osbourne performs with metal band Black Sabbath during the Ozzfest concert at the Meadowlands in East Rutherford, N.J., June 15, 1969. The band was formed in England in 1969 as bluesy Earth. It changed its name to Black Sabbath shortly after, adopting a quasi-occult, "evil" image, and went on to record and perform prolifically before disbanding in the late 1990s following multiple cast fall-outs and changes, having had great influence on other metal bands, notably Metallica.

Blondie

Blondie—fronted by Debbie Harry—at the Royal Albert Hall, London, November 23, 2005. Best known for the hit singles "Heart of Glass" ('79), "Call Me," and "The Tide is High" (both '80), and "Rapture" ('81), the band was formed in New York in 1974 as a splinter-group of the punk/sleaze outfit The Stilettoes.

Blood, Sweat & Tears

The 1960s-1970s band Blood, Sweat & Tears, with its leader, David Clayton-Thomas, in the center. The brass-rock band was formed in New York in 1967, and had a number of hits (including "You've Made Me So Very Happy," 1969) before dissolving in 1980.

The Blues Brothers

Jim Belushi performs as one of The Blues Brothers during halftime of Super Bowl XXXI, January 26, 1997, in New Orleans. Dan Aykroyd is in the background on the right. The R&B/blues band was set up in the late 1970s by comedians John Belushi (brother of Jim) and Dan Aykroyd and held a good account of themselves while performing with major rock and blues stars including Booker T. & The M.G.s, Paul McCartney's Wings, and Miles Davis. John Belushi performed as Joliet "Jake" Blues and Aykroyd as Elwood Blues, on stage and in hugely successful movies, while the band's album sales were prodigious. John Belushi died in 1982, but the band played on with various cast changes. (AP Photo via EMPICS)

Blur

Lead singer Damon Albarn of the Britpop band Blur performs at the Mayan Theater, Los Angeles, April 1, 1999, in a concert that was one of only two U.S. appearances the band made in support of its new album, the experimental "13." The band has had to adopt new styles at the demise of Britpop and, while it has been extremely successful in the UK, it has achieved only moderate U.S. chart placings, its best-selling album there being "Thinktank." (AP Photo via EMPICS)

Marc Bolan

British vocalist, guitarist, and composer Marc Bolan (right) is seen here with guest star David Bowie, recording his Granada TV show, "Marc," September 1977. Bolan formed acoustic folksy-rock duo Tyrannosaurus Rex (T.Rex) with Steve Peregrine Took in 1968 but died in 1977 in a Mini car that careered off the road while being driven by girlfriend, black American soul singer Gloria Jones.

Bon Jovi

Singer and guitarist Jon Bon Jovi (real name Bongiovi) performs at the Qwest Center in Omaha, Neb., as part of the "Have A Nice Day" Tour, November 12, 2005. The coiffured group was formed as a quintet in New Jersey in 1982/83 and joined the hard-rock touring scene, scoring in particular with the 1986 album "Slippery When Wet" and the single "Livin' On A Prayer," and the '88 album "New Jersey."   (AP Photo via EMPICS)

Boy George

Vocalist, composer, and producer Boy George in performance at the Virgin Megastore, London, March 2005, where he also signed copies of his of autobiography, "Straight." Born George Alan O'Dowd in London in June 1961, "New Romantic" George formed the group Culture Club with bassist Mickey Craig, drummer Jon Moss, and guitarist Roy Hay, and became best known for the singles "Do You Really Want To Hurt Me?" (1982) and "Karma Chameleon" (1983).

David Bowie

British singer David Bowie seen performing in Prague on June 23, 2004. Bowie was born in London in 1947 and has managed to achieve musical acclaim as a vocalist and composer with work as a producer and actor. Writing all his own songs (and many for others), arguably his best known works have been "Space Oddity" (about his astronaut "Major Tom") in 1969, "Fame" (1975), "Let's Dance" (1983), "Under Pressure" with Queen (1981), and "Dancing In The Street" with Mick Jagger (1985).

James Brown

James Brown was born in 1933 in rural poverty in Barnwell, South Carolina. He became an exciting vocalist, multi-instrumentalist, composer, and arranger, and had a string of hits in the 1960s, propelling him to the position as No. 1 black superstar and figurehead for American black consciousness movement. Justly acclaimed by his contemporaries, he has been a tireless R&B performer worldwide and prolific recording artist whose 1965 "I Got You (I Feel Good)" is testament to his greatness. Here, he performs at the Glastonbury Festival in England, June 2004.

The Carpenters

Karen and Richard Carpenter pose with their Grammys during the 14th annual Grammy Awards at New York's Felt Forum, March 14, 1972. The brother-sister duo, formed in 1969, won best pop vocal performance by a group for the album "The Carpenters." Their million-selling single "Close To You" set a pattern for a string of hit singles and albums until Karen died from a debilitating illness in 1983. (AP Photo via EMPICS)

The Cars

The Cars were formed in Boston, Mass., in 1976, with an original lineup of guitarist/vocalist Ric Ocasek, Ben Orr (bass/vocals), Greg Hawkes (keyboards/vocals/sax/percussion), Elliot Easton (guitar), and David Robinson (drums). Their easy-on-the-ear classic rock helped them achieve hits both sides of the Atlantic, particularly with the singles "Shake It Up" (1982) and "Drive" (1984). The band faded in 1987, and Orr sadly died in 2000. Photo shows the band in 1982. (AP Photo via EMPICS)

Johnny Cash

Legendary singer/songwriter and guitarist Johnny Cash performs at the Radio City Music Hall in New York, February 18, 1985. "The Man In Black" died in 2003 following a career lasting almost fifty years, during which he became most famed, influential, and loved for his country music performances and recordings, but also displayed his prodigious talents in cross-overs into rock 'n' roll, blues, rockabilly, folk and gospel. His rocky life story and the ups and downs of his career have been portrayed in the successful movie, "Walk The Line," released in 2005. (AP Photo via EMPICS)

Ray Charles

Legendary blues singer Ray Charles performs at the Apollo Theatre in Harlem, NYC, in "Blowin' the Blues Away," a gala benefit for Jazz at Lincoln Center, June 2, 2003. Born Ray Charles Robinson in Albany, Georgia, in 1930, he was blinded by glaucoma at age six yet still achieved acclaim as a true genius as vocalist, pianist, composer, and arranger, and particularly for his development of soul. He died June 10, 2004, leaving a fantastic legacy of his own songs and performances of others'. (AP Photo via EMPICS)

Cher

Singer Cher onstage at Wembley Arena, London, as part of her "Living Proof Farewell Tour" in 2004-5, although she continues to record and appear in movies. Born Cherilyn Sarkasian Cher in El Centro, California, in 1946, she has had a busy and successful musical career, first as a Phil Spector session singer, then as a duo with Sonny Bono, then as a solo artist regarded as the "high priestess of glam rock" and "dance-pop diva."

Chicago

Donnie Dacus, front row center, is introduced as the new lead guitarist of the rock group Chicago (originally formed in 1968) in Los Angeles, April 12, 1978. Dacus joins the group to replace the late Terry Kath, who died following an accidental gunshot. The other members are, back row from left: Brazilian percussionist Laudir De Oliveira, saxophonist Walter Parazaider, trumpet player and hornist Lee Loughnane, trombone player James Pankow, bass guitarist Peter Cetera, and drummer Danny Seraphine. Seated in the front row from left are: manager Herb Nanas, Dacus, and keyboarder Robert Lamm. The group retired in the early nineties. (AP Photo via EMPICS)

Eric Clapton

At Madison Square Garden in New York on October 24, 2005, acclaimed, peerless guitarist Eric Clapton performs in a reunion of the British band Cream he had formed in 1966 with vocalist Jack Bruce and drummer Ginger Baker. It was the band's first United States performance since their 1993 induction into the Rock 'n' Roll Hall of Fame. Self-taught musician Clapton enjoyed success with The Yardbirds, Derek & The Dominoes, Blind Faith and others, as well as having an influential on-off solo career punctuated with classics such as "Tears In Heaven," "Layla," "Knockin' On Heaven's Door," "Cocaine," and "Slowhand." (AP Photo via EMPICS)

The Clash

Members of the British rock band The Clash at a news conference at New York's Bond International Casino, May 31, 1981. A talented punk outfit, The Clash was formed in 1976 and had particular success with "Rock The Casbah" (1982) and "Should I Stay Or Should I Go" (1991) before disbanding in 1985. Band members shown are, from left, Joe Strummer, Paul Simonon, Topper Headon, and Mick Jones. (AP Photo via EMPICS)

Joe Cocker

British singer Joe Cocker performs during a concert in the garden of the "Landesmuseum" in Zurich, Switzerland, July 14, 2005. Born in 1944, Cocker has adopted hyper-energetic stage performances with emotion-charged recordings to forge critical acclaim among his peers (with whom he often performed) and the public internationally, in particular topping the charts with "Up Where We Belong" (with Jennifer Warnes) in 1983. (AP Photo via EMPICS)

Coldplay

Guy Berryman, Chris Martin, Jon Buckland, and Will Champion from British band Coldplay during rehearsals for a radio show in London. Formed in 1998 by university students, the post-Britpop, award-winning band found inspiration from, among others, Johnny Cash, U2, Jeff Buckley, and Oasis, are politically outspoken in performances (including such fund-raising concerts as Live 8), and have had chart success, in particular with "Parachutes" (2000) and "A Rush Of Blood To The Head" (2002).

Phil Collins

Former child actor and model, British singer Phil Collins, born in London in 1951, had great success as drummer/vocalist with chart-topping band Genesis in the 1980s, on top of many international solo hit singles ("Against All Odds," "Sussudio," "One More Night," "A Groovy Kind Of Love" and others), and has worked hard in support of charities such as Band Aid and Live Aid.

Sam Cooke

Definitive soul singer/songwriter Sam Cooke performs at a concert in New York's Copacabana nightclub. He was born Samuel Cook in Chicago in 1931 and died in a motel shooting in 1964, having built an influential career with such hits as "You Send Me," "Chain Gang," and "Twistin' The Night Away."
(AP Photo via EMPICS)

Elvis Costello

Elvis Costello performs at the New Orleans Jazz & Heritage Festival, April 30, 2005. Born Declan McManus in London in 1954, vocalist, guitarist, and composer Costello formed a permanent backing group, The Attractions, with whom he achieved country/rock cult following and chart successes in the late 1970s and '80s (particularly with "Oliver's Army"). Evolving a mix of sophisticated pop and elegant balladry, Costello has furthered his career with collaborations with Burt Bacharach and others.
(AP Photo via EMPICS)

Alice Cooper

Veteran American metal rock singer Vincent Furnier (born in Detroit, 1948) performing at the Hammersmith Apollo, London, May 2005. Furnier formed the band Alice Cooper (after several name changes) which eventually hit big with the most memorable "Killer" album (1971) and single/album "School's Out" (1972), enjoying notoriety for tongue-in-cheek ghoulish stage shows.

Creedence Clearwater Revival

Former Creedence Clearwater Revival front man John Fogerty, renowned for his bayou rock 'n' roll style, shown in May 1989. The group was formed in 1967 in California (although initially as a school group in 1959), and their output became massive sellers internationally during their 1969-1970 heyday. The band is probably best remembered for singles "Proud Mary" and "Bad Moon Rising" (both 1969). (AP Photo via EMPICS)

Crosby, Stills & Nash

David Crosby, Stephen Stills, and Graham Nash, from right to left, the legendary U.S. group, Crosby, Stills and Nash perform on the Auditorium Stravinski Hall stage during the 39th Montreux Jazz Festival, Switzerland, July 5, 2005. The group was formed in California in 1968, and combined soft-rock with slick vocal harmonies, a commercial mixture for a while. Later, along came Neil Young with chunky guitar and somber vocals to further the group's success, before they split and reformed in various lineups (again and again). (AP Photo via EMPICS)

Sheryl Crow

Easy-on-the-ear swing singer/songwriter Sheryl Crow performs on ABC's "Good Morning America" summer concert series in New York's Bryant Park, September 23, 2005, about the time when Crow's new album "Wildflower" went on sale. Born in Missouri in 1962, Crow is a classically trained musician who early in her career sang back-up to Rod Stewart, ex-Eagle Don Henley, and Joe Cocker before solo success came her way.
(AP Photo via EMPICS)

Cypress Hill

Members of American hip-hop, gangsta-rap band Cypress Hill performing on stage at the Glastonbury Music Festival 2000 in England. The band was formed in California in 1988, and has had most success with the album "Skull & Bones" released in April/May 2000.

Deep Purple

Ian Gillan, right, Steven Morse, left, and Ian Paice, center, of British rock group Deep Purple performing at the Eleftheria stadium, Nicosia, Cyprus, July 15, 2005. The group formed in London in 1968, their debut single "Hush" reaching high in the U.S. charts the same year. Profitable album sales followed, as did averagely successful singles, with their 1973 "Smoke On The Water" being most memorable. (AP Photo via EMPICS)

Def Leppard

Def Leppard lead singer Joe Elliot, who joined the British easy-listening metal band formerly known as Atomic Mass in 1977. Along with successful albums, the band has had high-charting singles such as "Hysteria," "Pour Some Sugar On Me," and "Love Bites" (all 1988).

Neil Diamond

Neil Diamond performs at the Quest Center in Omaha, Neb., as part of his 2005 tour, more than forty years after his recording debut in the early sixties. Classic singles have included "Sweet Caroline," "Cracklin' Rosie," "Song Sung Blue," "Love On The Rocks," and (with Barbra Streisand) "You Don't Bring Me Flowers." (AP Photo via EMPICS)

Diddy

Music mogul Diddy (aka Sean Combs) appears on stage during MTV's "Total Request Live" show at the MTV Times Square Studios, New York, December 1, 2005. Regarded as a major influence behind hip hop's commercial success, Diddy (born 1969) is a singer/rapper, songwriter, arranger, recording producer, actor and clothing designer. (AP Photo via EMPICS)

Celine Dion

Award-winning Canadian pop singer/songwriter and actress Celine Dion performs in The Theater at Madison Square Garden, NYC, October 15, 2004. Born in 1968, her "A New Day Has Come" is her most memorable among hugely popular international releases. She has worked generously in raising funds for victims of the Asian tsunami.
(AP Photo via EMPICS)

Dire Straits

British guitarist Mark Knopfler of Dire Straits plays his Gibson Les Paul guitar during the Live Aid concert for famine relief at Wembley Stadium, London, in 2005. The group was formed in 1977 and has had a string of singles and album hits with, in particular, "Sultans Of Swing," "Money For Nothing," "Love Over Gold," and "Brothers In Arms."

The Doobie Brothers

The classic rock group The Doobie Brothers pose in a New York hotel, September 18, 2000. The band was formed in 1970 in California and was at the height of its popularity during the next decade with such No. 1 hits as "Black Water" and "What A Fool Believes." From left are John McFee, Tom Johnston, Keith Knudsen, Patrick Simmons, and Michael Hossack. (AP Photo via EMPICS)

The Doors

Members of tempestuous and often lewd blues-rock band The Doors pose for a publicity photo. From left; John Densmore, Robby Krieger, Ray Manzarek and Jim Morrison. The band was formed in Los Angeles in 1965, "Light My Fire," "Hello I Love You," and "Waiting For The Sun" being the biggest-selling releases. Morrison died in 1971 at age 27.

The Drifters

More than fifty individuals in a constantly changing lineup worked with the official rock 'n' roll group that was formed in 1953 (several breakaway groups also exploited the name). This is a May 1971 photo. Most famous lead singer was Ben E. King and chart successes were highlighted by "There Goes My Baby," "Save The Last Dance For Me," and "Under The Boardwalk." (AP Photo via EMPICS)

Duran Duran

British pop-rock group Duran Duran's lead vocalist Simon Le Bon, left, and guitarist Andy Taylor sing together during the group's first concert in eighteen years in Tokyo, July 11, 2003. The band notched up huge chart successes in the 1980s with such singles as "Rio," "Is There Something I Should Know?" and "Wild Boys," before splitting in 1985, reforming again with various lineups, then splitting and reforming, with fans anticipating new releases in 2006. (AP Photo via EMPICS)

Bob Dylan

Bob Dylan performs at a festival in Jackson, Miss., May 17, 2003. Folk singer turned rock 'n' roll star, he was born Robert Allen Zimmerman in Minnesota in 1941, and has always been anti-establishment and often self-righteous and moralizing in his lyrics, while being a consummate concert performer and recording artist. He has scores of thinking-man's albums to his name, as well as high-charting singles, such as "Like A Rolling Stone" and "Lay Lady Lay." (AP Photo via

43

The Eagles

Timothy B. Schmit, Glenn Frey, Don Henley, and Joe Walsh from the California-formed megastar band The Eagles perform live on their 2004 "Farewell 1" Tour at the Coliseum, Hong Kong. During their heyday in the mid-1970s The Eagles were America's top-selling band of all time, notching up multimillion-selling singles and album hits with, for example, "One Of These Nights," "Lyin' Eyes," and "Hotel California," as well as undertaking grueling performance tours, which ultimately led to the band's demise in the early 1980s, with individual members going on to successful solo careers.

Earth, Wind And Fire

Earth, Wind And Fire perform at the Andre Agassi 10th Grand Slam For Children at the MGM Grand, Las Vegas, October 1, 2005. The band was formed as The Salty Peppers in Chicago in 1969, changing its name in 1970 and achieving moderate success until it had three soul/funk chart-topping albums in quick succession in 1975, before splitting in 1984.

Gloria Estefan

Gloria Estefan poses in New York after announcing her farewell "Live and Re-Wrapped Summer 2004 Tour." Cuban-born Estefan is an award-winning singer/songwriter and recording artist who has become a successful author. She had international hits in the mid-1980s with "Dr. Beat" and "Conga," suffered terrible injuries in a tour bus crash in 1990, but recovered to sell more than eight million copies of her 1993 "Mi Tierra," then began touring again in 1996.

Eminem

Eminem during the 11th annual MTV Europe Awards 2004 at the Tor di Valle in Rome, Italy. Born Marshall Bruce Mathers III in Missouri in 1972, Eminem has been a hugely successful rap artist for a decade, frequently appalling the international media and lots of mums and dads with lewd and violent lyrics, and in particular targeting the U.S. administration, while nevertheless banking millions made from record sales and energy-charged performances.

The Eurythmics

Dave Stewart and Annie Lennox, of the British duo Eurythmics, perform during the 33rd annual American Music Awards in Los Angeles, November 22, 2005. They actually formed the duo in 1976 as The Catch, then The Tourists, before settling on The Eurythmics in 1981. Chart-topping hits in the mid-eighties included "Sweet Dreams Are Made Of This" and "Sisters Are Doing It For Themselves" (with Aretha Franklin). (AP Photo via EMPICS)

Roberta Flack

Soul/jazz/folk singer Roberta Flack performs during the 39th Montreux Jazz Festival in Switzerland, July 14, 2005. She was born in North Carolina in 1937, and had big hits between 1970 and the early nineties, including "The First Time Ever I Saw Your Face," "Killing Me Softly With His Song," and "Set The Night To Music." (AP Photo via EMPICS)

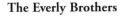

The Everly Brothers

The Everly Brothers, Don and Phil, perform on July 31, 1964. The influential, harmonizing duo had smash hits throughout the sixties, including "Bye Bye Love," "All I Have To Do Is Dream," and "Cathy's Clown," but acrimoniously split in 1973, to make up and reform for a triumphant world tour in 1985. (AP Photo via EMPICS)

Fleetwood Mac

The superstar rock group Fleetwood Mac, reuniting after thirteen years apart, performs during the American Gala evening at the Capital Center in Landover, Md., January 18, 1993, as a public rehearsal for the Presidential Gala. From left to right are John McVie, Stevie Nicks, Lindsey Buckingham, and Mick Fleetwood. The band was formed in 1967, have split and reunited a few times (with differing lineups), and have enjoyed critical acclaim and commercial success into the new millennium, with only John McVie and Mick Fleetwood remaining from the original band members. (AP Photo via EMPICS)

The Four Seasons

One of the greatest pop groups of all time, the harmonizing Four Seasons, fronted by Frankie Valli, had No. 1s with "Sherry," "Big Girls Don't Cry," "Walk Like A Man" and others in the early sixties, then again with "December '63 (Oh What A Night)" and "Grease" in the late seventies.

Foo Fighters

Drummer/vocalist/guitarist Dave Grohl fronts The Foo Fighters, the grunge-rock band he formed in Seattle in 1994 and with which he enjoyed good album sales, in particular with "One By One" in 2002.

The Four Tops

The legendary Motown singing group The Four Tops shown during a recording session in March 1986 in New York. Standing from left to right are Lawrence Payton, Levi Stubbs, Abdul "Duke" Fakir, and seated is Renaldo "Obie" Benson. One of their greatest hits was "Reach Out I'll Be There" in 1966.
(AP Photo via EMPICS)

Aretha Franklin

Regarded by many as the greatest female soul-stirrer of all, Tennessee-born (1942) Aretha Franklin warbles a few notes into microphone in January 28, 1972. She high-charted with "Respect" (1967), "Chain Of Fools" (1968), "Spanish Harlem" (1971), and "I Knew You Were Waiting (For Me)" (with George Michael, 1987).

Franz Ferdinand

Lead singer of post-punk, indie rock band Franz Ferdinand, Alex Kapranos, right, and singer/guitarist Nick McCarthy perform at Madison Square Garden, NYC, October 17, 2005. The Scottish band scored chart success with the eponymous debut album, and could be one to watch for the future. (AP Photo via EMPICS)

Garbage

Singer Shirley Manson of rock group Garbage performs on an open air stage in Budapest, Hungary, July 6, 2005. The band was formed in Wisconsin in 1994 and has achieved high chart successes with such singles as "#1 Crush" and "Stupid Girl." More in the pipeline, fans hope. (AP Photo via EMPICS)

Marvin Gaye

Motown vocalist, composer, keyboard player, and drummer Marvin Gaye performs at Radio City Music Hall, NYC, May 1983. He was born in Washington, DC, in 1939, had about thirty Top 50 hits during the decade after his breakthrough fourth single "Stubborn Kind Of Fellow" (1962), struck it big with "I Heard It Through The Grapevine" (1968), but was shot dead by his father in 1984.
(AP Photo via EMPICS)

Grand Funk Railroad

The rock group Grand Funk Railroad pose outside the West 72nd Street subway station in New York, April 11,1997. From left, Mel Schacher, Don Brewer, and Mark Farner. The Michigan-formed band was one of the most commercially successful American rock bands of the early 1970s, having to weather critical savagery before splitting in the early eighties.
(AP Photo via EMPICS)

Grateful Dead

Grateful Dead lead singer Jerry Garcia performs at the Oakland, California, Coliseum, November 1, 1992. The tight, raucous but melodic band, formed by Garcia in San Francisco in 1965, were prolific recording artists who took great pains to transfer their studio sound to their live act. Garcia died in 1995, and the band dissolved shortly after. (AP Photo via EMPICS)

Macy Gray

Ohio-born (as Natalie McIntyre, 1970) R&B singer and pianist Macy Gray performing during the Brit Awards 2000 ceremony in London. She has enjoyed charting with albums and singles, including "On How Life Is" and "I Try/I Try," respectively (both 1999).

Green Day

Green Day band members pose with their two awards during the MTV Europe Music Awards ceremony, November 3, 2005, in Lisbon, Portugal. The retro punk-rock band that was formed in California in the early 1990s has hit big in the U.S., particularly with the 1994-charting album "Dookie." (AP Photo via EMPICS)

Guns N' Roses

Controversy-bound heavy metal band Guns N' Roses, from left, Michael "Duff" McKagan, Dizzy Reed, Axl Rose, Saul "Slash" Hudson, and Matt Sorum, receive the Michael Jackson Video Vanguard Award for "November Rain" at the MTV Video Music Awards ceremony in Los Angeles, on September 9, 1992. The band was formed in California in 1985, but members have a history of falling out among themselves (and with almost everyone else except their cult following), with a potentially devastating internecine lawsuit filed in 2005. (AP Photo via EMPICS)

Bill Haley

First hero of rock 'n' roll, Bill Haley at the New Victoria Theatre in London, December 1976, where he appeared with his backing group, The Comets. Hitting big in the late 1950s and early 1960s, vocalist, guitarist, and composer Haley was born in Detroit in 1927 and sold nearly 70 million records, including chart-topping "Rock Around The Clock," before his death at age 54 in 1981.

Daryl Hall & John Oates

Vocalists, guitarists, and songwriters Daryl Hall (from Philadelphia), left, and John Oates (New York) pose before a performance at the Fleet Boston Pavilion in Boston, Mass., July 17, 2004. The soul/R&B duo first hit the charts in the mid-1970s with singles "Sara Smile," "She's Gone," and "Rich Girl," and had four No. 1s in the early-1980s, the best-known being "I Can't Go For That" and "Man Eater." Hall and Oates often worked apart and with top-selling bands, including The Temptations, and reformed in 1997 with moderate success. (AP Photo via EMPICS)

Heart

The folk-rock balladeer group Heart pose in Los Angeles, February 19, 1980. Bottom, left to right, are Nancy and Ann Wilson. Top row, left to right, are Steve Fossen, Michael Derosier, and Howard Leese. The band has scored with albums that have spawned high-charting singles, including "These Dreams," "Alone," and "All I Wanna Do Is Make Love To You." (AP Photo via EMPICS)

Jimi Hendrix

Vocalist and genius guitarist Jimi Hendrix was born in Seattle in 1942 and is seen here at the Isle of Wight (southern England) Festival shortly before he died in 1970 following years of incredibly hard touring, recording, and drink and drugs abuse. At times verging on the totally self-indulgent, Hendrix was the most influential rock guitarist of his generation, a master showman who exploited tricks such as playing his guitar behind his neck or with his teeth.

The Hollies

Formed in 1962 from members of two other groups, the British beat group The Hollies started out covering U.S. R&B numbers and hit big with catchy singles such as "Bus Stop," "Carrie-Anne," and the ballad "He Ain't Heavy He's My Brother." In 1968 founder-member guitarist/vocalist Graham Nash left to join forces with David Crosby and Stephen Stills to form Crosby, Stills & Nash, while his replacement, Terry Sylvester, is shown here (seated) being introduced by the rest of The Hollies.

Buddy Holly

One of the best-loved rock 'n' roll singers and guitarists of all time, Texas-born (1936) Buddy Holly had a brilliant career cut tragically short when he died in an air crash in 1959 at age 22. His legacy includes smash hits "That'll Be The Day," "Peggy Sue," "Oh Boy," and "It Doesn't Matter Anymore."

Whitney Houston

Multi-award winning, influential pop, R&B, soul singer Whitney Houston performs during Michael Jackson's "30th Anniversary Celebration, The Solo Years" concert at New York's Madison Square Garden, September 7, 2001. Born in New Jersey in 1963, she has been phenomenally successful with a string of international chart-toppers, including "Saving All My Love For You," "I Wanna Dance With Somebody," and "So Emotional," selling well over 100 million albums as well as holding down careers as record and film producer and actress.

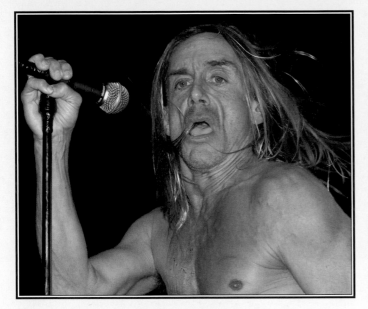

Iggy Pop

Iggy Pop & the Stooges onstage at the Carling Apollo Hammersmith, London, August 30, 2005, as part of ATP Concerts: Don't Look Back season. Born in Michigan in 1947, vocalist and composer Iggy Pop is often referred to as the "grandfather of punk" for his ranting, screaming, flailing, raucous stage performances.

INXS

The Australian rock band INXS (formed in 1979) pose for a group portrait in Aspen, Colorado, in 1997, with the late lead singer Michael Hutchence in the foreground. Hutchence, following years of drug abuse, was found hanging from a hotel room door in Sydney in 1997, leaving the band's international fans to replay hits such as "What You Need" and "Need You Tonight," while pondering what successes may have come the band's way had he not died.
(AP Photo via EMPICS)

Iron Maiden

Steve Harris and Dutch guitarist Janick Gers (right) of heavy metal band Iron Maiden performing on the Main Stage at the Reading Festival, England, August 28, 2005. The frenetic-energy, ear-booming, ghoul-image band was formed in 1977 by Harris and, following many personnel changes (Gers, for one, replacing another guitarist who had replaced another...), international touring, singles and album success came its way in the 1980s and continued through the nineties (with, for example, the hit single, "Bring Your Daughter To The Slaughter") into the new millennium.

The Jackson Five

Michael Jackson and his five brothers are seen together on the set of a Pepsi-Cola commercial. From left to right: Tito, Jermaine, Jackie, Michael, Randy, and Marlon Jackson. The all-singing, all-dancing group (somewhat unkindly regarded by many as the Black American answer to The Osmonds) was formed in 1966 and had four consecutive No. 1 singles in 1970 alone, including "I'll Be There," and remained one of the most popular groups before disbanding in 1990.

Michael Jackson

Enigmatic genius Michael Jackson, plagued for the last several years by legal problems related to accusations of child abuse, performs during his "Dangerous" tour in Bangkok in the early 1990s. Incomparably talented as a singer/songwriter and dance performer, and fabulously wealthy from his success, his image has been flawed.

Jane's Addiction

Perry Farrell (left), lead singer of always-controversial heavy metal/punk band Jane's Addiction, performing on the Main Stage at the Reading Festival, England, August 23, 2002. Formed by Farrell in California in 1984, the creative band had mainly album success, dissolved in the early 1990s, reformed ten years later, and broke up for good in 2004.

Jefferson Airplane/Starship

Members of the rock group Jefferson Airplane pose in San Francisco, March 8, 1968. From left are Marty Balin, lead singer, songwriter and founder; Grace Slick, vocalist; Spencer Dryden, drummer; Paul Kantner, electric guitar and vocalist; Jorma Kaukonen, lead guitarist, vocalist and songwriter; and Jack Casady, bass guitarist. The band was formed in California in early 1965 and became known for singing folk lyrics to rock beat. Chart-topping singles were "We Built This City" and "Nothing's Gonna Stop Us Now," but personnel changes and upsets caused the band to dissolve in the early 1970s, to be reformed in 1974 as Jefferson Starship, but it disbanded by 1990. (AP Photo via EMPICS)

Jethro Tull

Film actress Julie Ege presents a Gold Album on behalf of Warner Reprise to British Jethro Tull rock group, at London's Dorchester Hotel. Group members with her here are: John Evan (front row, left): Ian Anderson (front row, right), and back row (left to right): Martin Lancelot Barre, Jeffrey Hammond-Hammond, and Clive Bunker. The band was formed in 1968 and, influenced by classical and folk music, has achieved touring and record sales success both sides of the Atlantic, with founder/leader Anderson (vocalist, flute) saying in 2005 that he planned to tour with the band rather than create studio recordings.

Billy Joel

Billy Joel performs during a concert, January 23, 2006, at Madison Square Garden in New York. Born in Long Island in 1949, melodic pop/rock pianist/composer Joel has sold out eleven concerts at the Garden, breaking Bruce Springsteen's record of ten. He has had massive recording successes since the 1977-released album "The Stranger," as well as chart-topping singles that have included "It's Still Rock And Roll To Me," "Tell Her About It," and "We Didn't Start The Fire." (AP Photo via EMPICS)

Elton John

British vocalist, pianist, and composer Elton John performs during the 2005 Live 8 concert in London. Born in England in 1947, he has enjoyed fantastic success as a flamboyant showman and recording artist, and has become a truly great superstar who has poured money, time and influence into charitable causes, including The Elton John AIDS Foundation, earning a knighthood along the way. His adaptation of his own "Candle In The Wind," which he sang at Princess Diana's funeral in 1997, was recorded as a charity-contributor, was pushed to No. 1 by a Diana-adoring general public, and became possibly the biggest-selling single of all time.

Tom Jones

Superstar pop/rocker balladeer Tom Jones returns to the green, green, grass of home (Pontypridd, Wales) in 2005 for a one-off 65th birthday bash in front of 25,000-strong hometown crowd. His early hit "It's Not Unusual" (1965) displayed his powerful vocal style, paving the way for an enormous, eternal career that has spanned pop recording and sexy Las Vegas cabaret performances, revitalized from time to time with such nuggets as a creditable cover of Prince's "Kiss" in 2000.

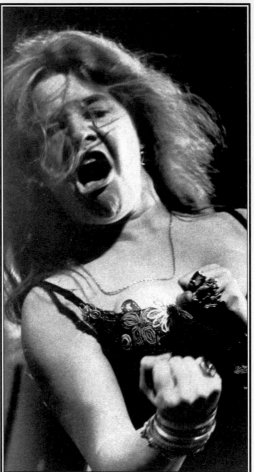

Janis Joplin

Blues/rock singer Janis Joplin performs with her band Big Brother and the Holding Company, July 29, 1968. Born in Texas in 1943, Joplin outgrew her raucous band for a solo career but her outrageous stage behavior led her into controversy, and off-stage she was no less wild, paying the price for over-indulgence in booze and drugs when she died in 1970 from a heroin overdose. She became a cult legend whose greatest hit, "Me And Bobby McGee," became a posthumous No. 1 in 1971. (AP Photo via EMPICS)

Judas Priest

British heavy metal band Judas Priest performs at the Tweeter Center in Mansfield, as part of its USA 2005 Tour. The high-energy, experimental band was formed in 1973, hit controversy with unproven accusations of including satanic material in its recordings, and has had influence on other metal bands such as Metallica.

Alicia Keys

Classically trained singer-songwriter and pianist Alicia Keys, born in Harlem, New York, in 1981, performing during The Prince's Trust Urban Music Festival, in London. Combining R&B, soul, funk and jazz in her stage and award-winning recording performances, Keys has become a noted record producer and actress who has worked actively for a wide variety of charities.

The Killers

Brandon Flowers of Las Vegas-formed synthesizing rock band The Killers performing on keyboards at the Glastonbury Festival, England, in 2005. The award-winning band has had hits both sides of the Atlantic, especially with "Mr. Brightside," heralding a potentially great, pure-21st century career.

The Kaiser Chiefs

Lead singer Ricky Wilson from The Kaiser Chiefs, the British post-punk award-winning band formed in early 2003, which has proven its talent in many international festival performances, including those for high-profile charities: definitely on the up.

B.B. King

Guitar maestro B.B. King performing part of his "B.B. King's Blues Festival 2004" event held at the Mountain Winery in Saratoga, August 4, 2004. Vocalist, guitarist, and composer, King (born in Mississippi in 1925) has dominated the blues scene for decades, was hugely influential on countless guitarists such as Eric Clapton, and remains revered by enthusiastic concert audiences

The Kinks

British pop band The Kinks backstage at the UK Music Hall Of Fame 2005, London, November 16, 2005. The band, formed in 1963 by brothers Ray and Dave Davies, had huge following in both the U.S. and UK in the 1960s and through the '70s with such hits as "You Really Got Me," "All Day And All Of The Night," "Tired Of Waiting For You," "Dedicated Follower Of Fashion," and "Lola."

Kiss

The rock band Kiss, from left, Gene Simmons, Tommy Thayer and Paul Stanley, at the PNC Bank Arts Center in Holmdel, N.J., July 20, 2004. The grease-painted, gothic-style band, formed in New York in 1971, wowed rock fans with explosive stage performances and high-charting singles and albums in its 1970s heyday, but dropped the garish image in the mid-1980s to muted appreciation until achieving chart success again in 1990 with "Forever."

Gladys Knight

Child prodigy Gladys Knight was born in Atlanta in 1944, and was singing with a gospel group when only four. The family group Gladys Knight And The Pips was formed when she was just eight and had huge hits in the 1970s and 1980s with singles such as "Every Beat Of My Heart," "Midnight Train To Georgia," and "The Best Thing That Ever Happened To Me." Knight launched a successful and award-winning solo R&B singing career in the late 1980s, has regularly performed in her own Las Vegas show, and become a TV celebrity.

LL Cool J

LL Cool J ("Ladies Love Cool James") was born James Todd Smith in Long Island in 1968 and has appeared, wearing a hat as trademark, under many different names. Hip hop acts almost invariably have short careers, but master rapper LL has been the exception, with great recording success mixed with award-winning performances in movies, as well as a long-running TV sitcom.

Cyndi Lauper

Superlative singles "Girls Just Want To Have Fun," "Time After Time," and "True Colors" (spawned from highly rated and successful albums) propelled New York-born (1953) Cyndi Lauper as a chart-hitting singer/songwriter in the 1980s and 1990s. Into the new millennium she has continued to record and has built a movie acting career.

Led Zeppelin

Led Zeppelin were the best rock band ever, they lived the life-style, of sex, drugs and booze, and one of them paid the price. Drummer John Bonham died in 1980 from an alcohol binge. Zeppelin sold over 300 million albums worldwide, a third of those in the USA. The photo shows three of the band, (L-R) John Bonham, Robert Plant, and Jimmy Page with Sandy Denny.

Linkin Park

Formed initially as Hybrid Theory in Los Angeles in 1999, hip hop/rock/metal band Linkin Park high-charted with its debut album "Hybrid Theory" in 2000, then chart-topped in 2003 with "Meteora," and has gone on to win a coveted Grammy award for Best Hard Rock Performance for "Crawling."

Little Richard

There has seldom been a decade since his musical career began in 1951 in which Little Richard (born Richard Wayne Penniman in Georgia in 1935) has failed to bask in some limelight. The gospel/rock 'n' roll vocalist, pianist, and composer first charted heavily in 1955 with his debut release "Tutti Frutti," following up rapidly with gems like "Long Tall Sally," "Lucille," "Good Golly Miss Molly," and "The Girl Can't Help It." He has since seen good and lean times, continuing to record and to perform often as a guest artist: he even performed at Bill Clinton's presidential inauguration in 1993.

Jennifer Lopez

Singer and actress Jennifer Lopez (J-Lo) was born in the The Bronx, NYC, in 1970, and began her artistic career as a stage musicals dancer, moving onto small acting roles in TV series and films before her big break in 1997 playing the lead role in the biopic movie "Selena." Her debut Latin pop album "On The 6" was released in 1999, since when she has had chart-topping success with the album "J. Lo" in 2001 and single "This Is Me … Then" in 2002, with plenty more in the pipeline.

Lynyrd Skynyrd

The Florida country/Southern blues/rock band Lynyrd Skynyrd was formed initially as My Backyard by Ronnie Van Zant in 1966 and released its debut album "Pronounced Leh-nerd Skin-nerd, " containing the charting "Free Bird" single in 1974. The continuously touring band was involved in an airplane crash in 1977 that claimed the lives of Van Zant and others. While it was reformed in 1979, the band dissolved again, although in 1987 it regrouped for a memorial tour and release of the album "Southern By The Grace Of God," (1988), then split again, reformed again in 1991, releasing further albums throughout the 1990s and early 2000s.

Madness

Formed in 1979
from ska band The
Invaders, the British
ska/pop/R&B band
was enormously
successful
throughout the
early-mid 1980s
with singles such as
"It Must Be Love,"
"House of Fun,"
and "Our House"
(which marked a
U.S. breakthrough),
but split in 1986,
reforming
occasionally for one-
off sell-out shows.

Madonna

Born Madonna Ciccone in Michigan in 1961, singer/songwriter Madonna is regarded as the first true female star of rock music, having been phenomenally successful in single and album releases, as well as on the rock stage and as an actress (in the acclaimed move "Evita"), since her first real hit, "Holiday," in 1983. She has enjoyed numerous No. 1s (including "Like A Virgin," "Material Girl," "Papa Don't Preach," and "Justify My Love"), and has endured and evolved into a mega superstar.

Bob Marley

Vocalist and composer Bob Marley was born in Jamaica in 1945 and became the most influential figure in the development of reggae music, full of both social and political comment, but melodic too. Unforgettable numbers included "I Shot The Sheriff" and "No Woman No Cry." Marley died in 1981.

Meat Loaf

Surging, soaring but melodic "Bat Out Of Hell" single and album (which also included strident but tuneful singles "Two Out Of Three Ain't Bad" and "Dead Ringer For Love") shook up the punk/new wave music scene of the late 1970s/early 1980s, forcefully reminding it of hard rock's presence, but also crossing-over into pop appreciation. Its perpetrator, Meat Loaf (born Marvin Lee Aday in Texas in 1948), adopted a tumultuous theatricality, which should have surprised nobody since he had already starred in the movie "Rocky Horror Picture Show." He's still rockin' today.

Men At Work

The Australian band Men At Work encompassed passionate pop and new wave to sprint up the charts in 1981 and stayed there for three years with record-breaking albums such as its debut "Business As Usual," winning a Grammy for Best New Group in 1982.

Metallica

California band Metallica, formed by Lars Ulrich in 1981, with a mix of thrash metal and hard rock, has become the most commercially successful of all heavy metal bands, surviving tragedy and multiple lineup changes and thriving in the new millennium with sell-out tours (such as the Madly In Anger With The World Tour of 2004, shown) and high-charting singles and albums (more than 90 million sold worldwide).

George Michael

George Michael (born Georgios Panayatiou in London, 1963) had tumultuous success in the mid-1980s with duo Wham! (with Andrew Ridgeley), scored solo hit singles with "Different Corner" and "Careless Whisper," then split from the duo for a chart-topping solo career that has delighted fans with such albums (and singles from them) as "Ladies And Gentlemen" (1998) and "Songs From The Last Century" (1999).

Kylie Minogue

The hugely successful Australian singer/songwriter, pop star, sex symbol and actress Kylie Minogue performs at the Hallenstadium in Zurich, Switzerland, June 6, 2002. A truly international chart-topper, her biggest U.S. successes to date have been the singles "The Locomotion" and "Can't Get You Out Of My Head." In 2006 she was reported to be responding well to treatment for breast cancer. (AP Photo via EMPICS)

Joni Mitchell

Folk/pop/jazz vocalist, guitarist, pianist, and composer Joni Mitchell was born Roberta Joan Anderson in Alberta, Canada, in 1943. Her big year was 1974, with the release of charting single "Help Me" and albums "Court And Spark" and "Miles Of Aisles," and she has continued to record and tour successfully through to the 2000s. In 2002 she received a Grammy award for being "one of the most important female recording artists of the rock era."

Moby

Electronic performer Moby was born Richard Melville Hall in New York in 1965, has been a DJ, is a vocalist, keyboard player and guitarist, has released singles and albums under a variety of names (including Voodoo Child and DJ Cake), has seen his songs adopted for movies and commercials, and has had chart-topping success both sides of the Atlantic, particularly with "Play" and "18."

Moody Blues

The British pop/rock/progressive band Moody Blues was formed in 1964 and is best known for the classic mega-hit singles "Go Now" (1964) and "Nights In White Satin" (1967, 1972, and 1979). Following various "rests" (splits) from touring and recording, and lineup changes, the band endured into the new millennium with a solid but aging fan base.

The Monkees

While rock aficionados might sneer at the 1965-formed The Monkees, there's no denying the pop success of the heavily marketed American answer to The Beatles: in a very short career the band had three No.1 and several other high-charting singles in the 1960s (including "I'm A Believer") enjoyed a highly successful TV series as well as follow-up album releases into the 1980s, before splitting and reforming, finally working together again in 2001.

Alanis Morissette

Canadian pop/rock singer/songwriter Alanis Morissette was born in Ottawa in 1974 and had a massive hit with her debut international album "Jagged Little Pill" in 1995, followed by other U.S. chart-toppers in 1998 and 2002, and hit singles from the albums. She continues to record, and has pursued a career as a movie actress and TV personality.

Van Morrison

Vocalist, composer, and multi-instrumentalist Van Morrison was born George Ivan in Belfast, Northern Ireland, in 1945, and was initially influenced by his parents' interest in American Deep South blues, emerging in the 1970s and 1980s as a major influential force among R&B and Celtic soul concert and recording performers. His most successful singles have included "Brown-Eyed Girl" and "Have I Told You Lately," while his albums (including "Moondance") throughout a four-decade career have been well received.

Motörhead

High-energy British metal band Motörhead was formed in 1975 and, with varying lineups, has established a fanatical following for its (extremely) loud tour performances and recordings, the biggest of which have been "Motörhead (live)" and "Ace Of Spades," while having heavy influence on many contemporary punk, heavy metal, and rock 'n' roll bands.

Muse

The British alternative rock band Muse (formed 1994) during a Glastonbury Festival, England, performance. In recent years the politically controversial band has toured extensively internationally and has consistently charted with singles and albums in the UK, breaking into the U.S. listings with "Hysteria" (2004) and "Stockholm Syndrome" (2005).

*NSYNC

The harmonizing, five-guy *NSYNC pop band was formed in Florida in 1996 and has internationally record-breaking singles and albums to its credit (its eponymous debut album reaching No. 2). While originally considered merely a "boy band," *NSYNC has become an acclaimed singing/songwriting band that continues to record and tour, with individual members also pursuing solo music and acting careers.

Nelly

Hip hop singer Nelly (born Cornell Haynes, Jr., in Texas in 1974) arrives at the 2nd annual "Fashion Rocks" Party & Concert to benefit victims of the 2005 destructive Hurricane Katrina. Nelly attained stardom in 2000 and has become a triple Grammy Award winner, while achieving No. 1 album and single successes with "Suit" and "Shake Ya Tailfeather," respectively, in 2004, and "Grillz" in 2006.

Rick Nelson

Born Eric Hilliard Nelson in New Jersey in 1940, Rick Nelson, vocalist, composer, guitarist, and actor, left a huge legacy of late-1950s/early-1960s) hit singles (including "Poor Little Fool" and "Hello Mary Lou") when he was killed in an air crash in 1985.

Nickelback

Canadian hard rock, post-grunge band Nickelback was formed in 1995 and has produced high-charting albums (such as "The State") and singles (like "How You Remind Me"). Critics may deplore the band's use of digital processing during recording, but the bank manager's happy!

Nine Inch Nails

Trent Reznor, lead singer of the American industrial rock band Nine Inch Nails, performing at the Glastonbury Music Festival 2000 in England. The band was formed by Reznor in California in 1989 and has focused on such happy subjects as torture, masochism, and killing, which seems to have gone down well with fans, judging by the success of such albums as "The Downward Spiral."

Nirvana

A most influential grunge rock band, Nirvana was formed in Washington State in 1987 by frontman Kurt Cobain, who committed suicide in 1994 following years of illness. The band had run up massive recording and touring successes by then, and its popularity even grew in the years that followed, with the release of several albums, including "Unplugged In New York."

Notorious B.I.G.

Born Christopher George Latore Wallace in New York in 1972, and also known as Biggie Smalls, hip hop singer Notorious B.I.G. is regarded as a legendary rapper, whose highest record sales were achieved following his death from a shooting in Los Angeles in 1997. Biggie was himself suspected of involvement of the murder in 1994 of rap star Tupac Shakur.

Oasis

Liam Gallagher, lead singer and songwriter with the Britpop/alternative rock group Oasis, performs at The Palace of Auburn Hills, Michigan, August 30, 1996. The band was formed in the early 1990s and soared to the top of international charts, scoring particularly highly with albums in the U.S. such as "(What's The Story) Morning Glory?" and "Be Here Now." Personnel changes have meant that only Liam and his brother Noel remain from the original lineup. (AP Photo via EMPICS)

The O'Jays

The O'Jays during a taping of "Motown Live" in September 9, 1998. Three decades after singing that money was "the root of all evil," the Philadelphia soul group, actually formed in Ohio in 1958, had a string of hit singles in the 1970s, including "For The Love Of Money." Ironically, The O'Jays lost a bid to block its former record label, Philadelphia International Records, from cashing in on songs the group recorded in the early 1980s, but didn't think were good enough to release. (AP Photo via EMPICS)

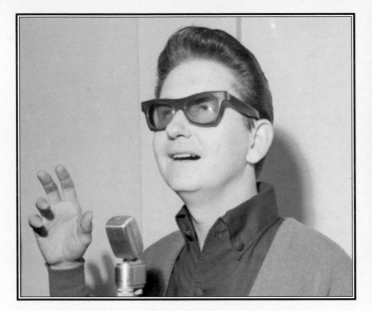

Roy Orbison

Influential singer/songwriter and guitarist Roy Orbison had a fabulously successful music career of more than thirty years before dying of a heart attack in 1988. Born in Texas in 1936, he high-charted regularly during the early-mid-1960s with such classics as "Only The Lonely," "Running Scared," and "Oh Pretty Woman," but suffered tragedies (wife killed in road accident, 1966; two sons killed in a fire, 1968) before going on to further, lower-key success during the 1970s and early '80s.

The Osmonds

The Osmonds perform during a 1995 Christmas show at the Osmond Family Theater in Branson, Mo. In the early 1970s the sugar-sweet family group had top- and high-charting singles (including "One Bad Apple" and "Love Me For A Reason"), but when their popularity waned individual members (notably Donny and Marie) pursued successful solo careers that persist today. (AP Photo via EMPICS)

Pet Shop Boys

Singer Neil Tennant and keyboarder Chris Lowe (background) of the British electronic pop duo Pet Shop Boys perform during an AIDS gala in Berlin. The duo was formed in 1983 and in 1985 achieved a worldwide No. 1 with "West End Girls" single, going on to feature regularly in U.S. dance and club charts. They still record and tour today.

Tom Petty

Florida singer/songwriter and guitarist Tom Petty linked up with The Heartbreakers in 1976 and had recording and touring successes on both sides of the Atlantic during the late 1970s and early 1980s, before soloing over the next few years and occasionally working with the band again, and also with The Traveling Wilburys. Petty has also made movies and has hosted his own TV show.

Pink

Born Alecia Beth Moore in Pennsylvania in 1979, pink-haired, soulful-sounding singer/songwriter Pink is definitely a girl of the 21st century who has scored big with albums such as "M!issundaztood" (2001) and particularly the single "Lady Marmalade," with which she collaborated with Christina Aguilera. Mya, and Lil' Kim.

Pink Floyd

Left to right, Dave Gilmour, Nick Mason, and Roger Waters of British rock band Pink Floyd performing during the 2005 Live 8 concert. The band has endured despite splits and reformations since its formation in 1965, being best known for "Dark Side Of The Moon" (1973) and "The Wall" (1979).

Elvis Presley

Elvis Presley, the King of Rock, showing signs of illness and over-indulgence in Providence, R.I., on May 23, 1977, three months before his death. Regarded as the major influence on later rock stars, his success was phenomenal during his lifetime and after with the release of compilations and the odd hit single.
(AP Photo via EMPICS)

Prince

Prince arrives in New York for a party celebrating the release of his new album "Musicology," April 20, 2004. Born Prince Rogers Nelson in Minneapolis in 1958, the flamboyant funk, pop, rock vocalist/guitarist and composer has notched up No. 1 albums (including "Purple Rain" and "Batman") as well as singles (including "When Doves Cry" and "Let's Go Crazy") throughout a musical career that has lasted more than thirty years.
(AP Photo via EMPICS)

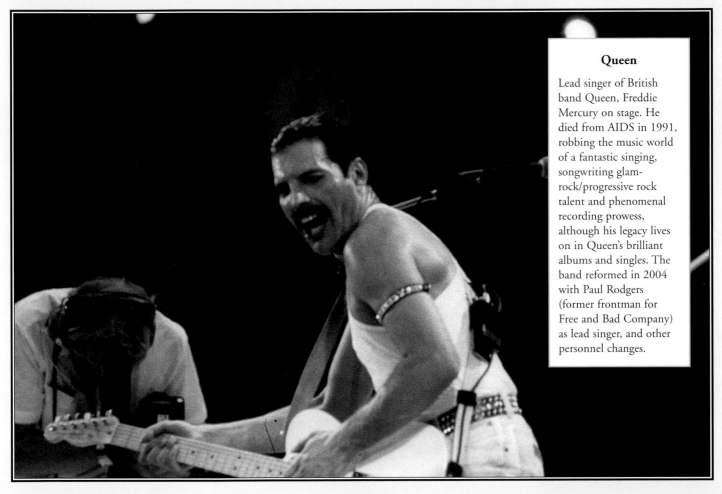

Queen

Lead singer of British band Queen, Freddie Mercury on stage. He died from AIDS in 1991, robbing the music world of a fantastic singing, songwriting glam-rock/progressive rock talent and phenomenal recording prowess, although his legacy lives on in Queen's brilliant albums and singles. The band reformed in 2004 with Paul Rodgers (former frontman for Free and Bad Company) as lead singer, and other personnel changes.

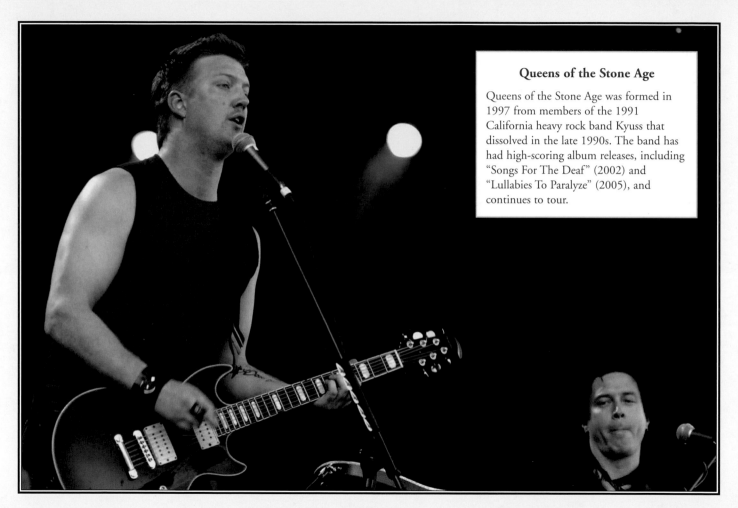

Queens of the Stone Age

Queens of the Stone Age was formed in 1997 from members of the 1991 California heavy rock band Kyuss that dissolved in the late 1990s. The band has had high-scoring album releases, including "Songs For The Deaf" (2002) and "Lullabies To Paralyze" (2005), and continues to tour.

Radiohead

Members of the British alternative rock band Radiohead first got together at school in the mid-1980s, but finished their formal education and re-emerged in 1991 to gig, produce demo tapes, and record, but had to wait until 1993 for international success with the re-release of the single "Creep," following up between 1997 and 2003 with massive album hits "OK Computer," "Kid A," "Amnesiac," and "Hail To The Thief."

Ramones

Members of the New York new wave, punk rock group Ramones (Richie Ramone, top left, Joey Ramone, top right, Dee Dee Ramone, bottom left, and Johnny Ramone, bottom right, all of whom adopted "Ramone" as a working surname) shown in 1986. The band was enormously influential in the foundation of punk but split in 1996.

Razorlight

Razorlight performs at the Live 8 concert in London, July 2, 2005, part of a series of free concerts held around the world designed to press leaders of the rich G8 countries to help impoverished African nations. Razorlight is a post-punk/new wave band formed in 2002, and has gained success in the UK charts, but the jury's out so far as to whether it can break into the U.S. market. (AP Photo via EMPICS)

Red Hot Chilli Peppers

California funk-rock rapcore band the Red Hot Chilli Peppers with the "Pushing the Envelope" award they received at the My VH1 Awards 2000, at the Shrine Auditorium in Los Angeles. The band's best-selling studio albums have included "Blood Sugar Sex Magik," "One Hot Minute," "Californication," and "By The Way."

Lou Reed

Influential singer/songwriter and guitarist Lou Reed takes the podium as Velvet Underground, the group he once headed, is inducted into the Rock and Roll Hall of Fame in New York, January 17, 1996. Bandmate John Cale is at left, and at right is Martha Morrison, accepting for late band member Sterling Morrison. The band folded in 1973, while Reed had left in 1970 and began a solo career in 1972, achieving a hit with "Walk On The Wild Side." (AP Photo via EMPICS)

R.E.M.

A melodic and experimental alternative rock band formed in Georgia in 1980/81, R.E.M. has long been critically acclaimed and influential through touring performances and trans-Atlantic chart-topping albums such as "Out Of Time" (1991) and "Monster" (1994). Vociferous on AIDS and environmental issues, the band performed during the 2005 Live 8 concert.

Lead singer Kevin Cronin of REO Speedwagon performs at JFK Stadium in Philadelphia during the Live Aid famine relief concert, July 13, 1985. The Illinois rock band released its eponymous debut album in 1971, peaked in popularity in 1985 with the chart-topping single "Can't Fight This Feeling," has released several compilation albums, and has continued to tour during the new millennium while also promising further album releases. (AP Photo via EMPICS)

Lionel Richie

Easy listening vocalist, pianist, composer, producer Lionel Richie performs in front of many thousands of Hungarians during his concert in Budapest, June 26, 2005, some twenty years after his heyday that saw him regularly chart-topping with albums such as "Can't Slow Down" and hit singles like "Say You, Say Me." Born in Alabama in 1949, Richie fronted for the Motown band The Commodores during the 1970s, but quit to build a megastar solo career in 1981. (AP Photo via EMPICS)

Smokey Robinson

Kicking off his silver anniversary in music with a two-night, standing-room-only engagement, Motown singer/songwriter and record producer Smokey Robinson, left, is joined by friend and fellow entertainer Berry Gordy at the Greek Theater in Los Angeles, June 15, 1981. Gordy was president and founder of Motown Records, for which Robinson recorded from the early 1960s, first as The Miracles then as high-charting solo artist. Composer of scores of hit songs, Robinson still tours periodically, and released a gospel album, "Food For The Spirit," in 2004. (AP Photo via EMPICS)

The Righteous Brothers

The Righteous Brothers, Bobby Hatfield, left, and Bill Medley, perform before being inducted into the Rock and Roll Hall of Fame, March 10, 2003, in New York. Hatfield died from a drug overdose that same year. The duo's first big hit was "You've Lost That Lovin' Feeling" in 1965. (AP Photo via EMPICS)

The Rolling Stones

Ron Wood, Keith Richards, Mick Jagger and Charlie Watts, from left, of The Rolling Stones, performing at the Charlotte Bobcats Arena in Charlotte, NC, October 21, 2005. Formed in the early 1960s, the British band, with varying lineups, has been regarded as the greatest rock group ever and is still touring and releasing records despite coming up to pensionable age. (AP Photo via EMPICS)

Linda Ronstadt

Country rock singer/songwriter Linda Ronstadt performing at the 20th annual Country Music Association awards show in Nashville, Tenn., October 13, 1986. Born in Arizona in 1946, the award-winning Ronstadt was at her peak in the late 1970s and early 1980s, with chart-topping singles such as "You're No Good" and "When Will I Be Loved" as well as a string of successful albums, including "Simple Dreams" and "Living In The U.S.A." (AP Photo via EMPICS)

Diana Ross

Superstar singer and actress Diana Ross, former lead singer of the legendary The Supremes, performs at the start of the Live at Sunset Festival in Zurich, Switzerland, July 17, 2005. Her massively successful solo career has spawned No.1s such as "Reach Out And Touch (Somebody's Hand)," "Ain't No Mountain High Enough," and "Do You Know Where You're Going To," and she continues to tour and release recordings almost forty years after she left The Supremes in 1970. (AP Photo via EMPICS)

Roxy Music

Bryan Ferry of the influential British art rock band, Roxy Music. The band was successful during the 1970s (with and without early member, synthesizer Brian Eno), informally dissolved in 1976 while Ferry went solo, then reformed in 1978, split again, to reform for a tour in 2001, and were releasing recordings four-five years later.

Run-D.M.C.

Rap trio Run-D.M.C. pose on a New York City stoop, April 5, 2001. From left are Jam Master Jay (Jason Mizell), DMC (Darryl McDaniels), and DJ Run (Jason Simmons). The once-mighty rap pioneers were attempting a comeback with their new album "Crown Royal," before Jam Master Jay was shot dead in a New York recording studio in October 2002. (AP Photo via EMPICS)

Carlos Santana

Born in Mexico in 1947, Carlos Santana attained critical acclaim as a guitarist fusing salsa, rock, blues and jazz even before his 1969 debut album "Santana," which sold over a million copies in the U.S. alone. Probably his best known single has been "Black Magic Woman," chased closely by "She's Not There." His biggest album to date has been the 1999 "Supernatural," produced in collaboration with Eric Clapton and others.

Rush

The Canadian progressive rock band Rush was formed in Ontario in 1968 and has become one of the biggest selling rock bands, having scored heavily with albums such as "Counterparts" (1993) and "Test For Echo" (1996). The band continues to tour and release albums.

Seal

British soul singer Seal was born Seal Samuel in England in 1963, his first, eponymous, album being released in 1991, followed by another self-titled album in 1994, spawning the single "Kiss From A Rose," which when re-released in 1995 following its featuring in the soundtrack of the movie "Batman Forever" topped the charts in the U.S. and elsewhere.

Neil Sedaka

Rock Star? Hardly. But influential singer/songwriter, pianist, and pop recording artist, definitely. Neil Sedaka has enjoyed ups and downs during a music career of more than forty years, with early successes including the top-charting "Breaking Up Is Hard To Do" (unusually reworked fourteen years later and reaching No. 8), "Laughter In The Rain," and "Bad Blood." He has written (initially with Howard Greenfield, later with Phil Cody) very many hit songs for a variety of other performers, including Abba, and in 2005 scored a remarkable No. 1 again (in the UK) as the writer of Tony Christie's "Amarillo," which featured in a multi-celebrity comical video. (AP Photo via EMPICS)

Bob Seger

Born in Michigan in 1945, Bob Seger took a long time to become an overnight success, starting out in the early 1960s and finally charting (with backing group The Silver Bullet Band) with "Live Bullet" in 1976, followed quickly by "Night Moves," "Stranger In Town" (spawning single "Hollywood Nights"), and the 1980 No. 1 album "Against The Wind." Seger's hard-rocking but melodious music propelled him into the Rock and Roll Hall of Fame in 2005, while fans were waiting anxiously for a planned new album release.

The Sex Pistols

The British punk rock band The Sex Pistols debut in the United States with a performance in Atlanta, January 5, 1978. At center stage is the band's frontman Johnny Rotten as he sips refreshment during the show. From left are bass player Sid Vicious (who died of a drugs overdose in New York in 1979 while out on bail facing a murder charge); Paul Cook, drums; and Steve Jones, guitar. Formed in 1975, the band will be remembered more for its obnoxious behavior than its music. (AP Photo via EMPICS)

Shaggy

Reggae singer Shaggy poses for the media during a photocall in Monte Carlo, ahead of the 2002 World Music Awards. Born Orville Richard Burrell in Kingston, Jamaica, in 1968, Shaggy moved to New York with his parents and joined the US Marine Corps in 1988, serving in Iraq. He left the service to pursue a music career, scoring heavily with the albums "Boombastic" in 1995 and "Hot Shot" (No. 1 in 2000).

Shakira

Colombia's Shakira performs at Z100's Jingle Ball 2005 held at the Madison Square Garden in New York. The talented Latin singer/songwriter (born in 1977) has achieved success in her native language, and also worldwide with translations, and was a Grammy Award winner for Best Latin Rock Album for "Fijación Oral Vol. 1," while her English-language "Oral Fixation Vol. 2" charted in the U.S. and elsewhere.

Simon & Garfunkel

Paul Simon, right, and Art Garfunkel perform in Madison Square Garden, New York, December 2, 2003, during their first concert tour together in twenty years. Together, the multi-award-winning duo had a string of hits in the late 1960s/early '70s, including "The Sound Of Silence," "Mrs. Robinson," and "Bridge Over Troubled Water," before splitting a couple of times to pursue successful solo projects, and then reforming. (AP Photo via EMPICS)

Carly Simon

Born in New York in 1945, vocalist/songwriter Carly Simon is probably best known for her singles "You're So Vain" (No. 1 in 1972) and "Nobody Does It Better" (No. 2 in 1977), although she has had subsequent successes, including the high-charting album "Moonlight Serenade" in 2005.

Simple Minds

Scottish new wave/alternative rock band Simple Minds has been around a long time but, although it has had European success, it is having to push hard to follow up its only U.S. charting number, "Don't You (Forget About Me)", which got to No. 1 in 1985.

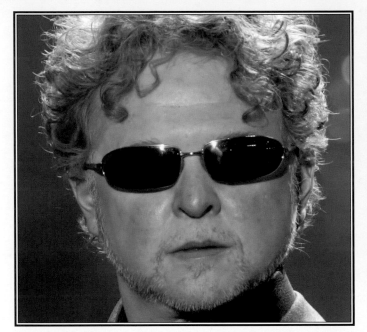

Simply Red

Founder and lead singer/songwriter of British band Simply Red, Mick Hucknall performs during a German TV show on October 1, 2005. Simply Red, already popular in the UK, first hit the U.S. charts big time with the single "Holding Back The Years" in 1985, followed by "If You Don't Know Me By Now" in 1989, and the album "Stars" in 1991. (AP Photo via EMPICS)

Percy Sledge

Soul legend Percy Sledge was born in Alabama in 1941 and, although he displayed superb vocal artistry in a number of appreciated singles and albums, it is for his 1966 No. 1 classic "When A Man Loves A Woman" that he is best remembered, especially since it was adopted for a Levi's jeans advert some twenty years later, thus making it a hit all over again.

Sly And The Family Stone

Sly Stone (born Sylvester Steward in Texas, 1944) set up the multi-cultural, dual-sex, rock/soul/funk band Family Stone in California in 1966, combining punchy brass riffs and soaring rock guitar with wild vocal harmonies and strident dance beat. Initial success came in 1968 with the single "Dance To The Music," charting at No.8, followed by the 1969 No. 1 "Everyday People," and further chart-toppers, including "Thank You (Falettinme Be Mice Elf Agin)" (1970) and "Family Affair" (1971). The band dissolved in 1975 after escalating drug abuse, personnel clashes and lineup changes.

Snoop Dogg

Hip hop rapper artist Snoop Dogg (born Cordozar Calvin Broadus, Jr, in California, 1971) seen during a memorial service for executed murderer Stanley "Tookie" Williams, December 20, 2005, in South Los Angeles. Snoop Dogg has had several No. 1 albums, including "Doggystyle" (1993), and the chart-topping single "Drop It Like It's Hot" (2004). (AP Photo via EMPICS)

Britney Spears

Louisiana singer/songwriter Britney Spears at the Billboard Awards, Las Vegas, December 8, 2004. Spears has enjoyed phenomenal recording and touring success, being one of the top selling female artists of all time. She has sold millions of albums, singles (including "....Baby One More Time"), and DVDs. (AP Photo via EMPICS)

The Spice Girls

Top-selling all-female group ever, The Spice Girls perform at the Brit Awards ceremony, London, February 24, 1997. Most active between 1996 (when the group released its No. 1 eponymous debut album) and 2000 (with the high-charting "Forever" album), the group has sold more than 75 million records, including a string of hit singles (among them "Wannabe," "Say You'll Be There," and "2 Become 1"). The group has never formally split, although there appears little chance of a comeback, while individual members have pursued solo careers.

Dusty Springfield

Born Mary O'Brien in London in 1939, Dusty Springfield (formerly of the folk-pop trio The Springfields) became a highly acclaimed soul/pop solo singer who (unusually for a British female artist) made it big both sides of the Atlantic, with five high-charting singles in the U.S., including "Wishin' And Hopin'" (1964) and "You Don't Have To Say You Love Me" (1966). After her career had faded by the 1970s she hit the charts again as a guest vocalist with The Pet Shop Boys ("What Have I Done To Deserve This?" in 1987, and the 1989 singles "Nothing Has Been Proved" and "In Private"). Sadly, Dusty died from cancer in 1999.

Bruce Springsteen

Bruce Springsteen in concert in Gothenburg, Sweden, June 23, 2005, on the unplugged "Devils & Dust Tour." Born in New Jersey in 1949, politically active Springsteen blasted to prominence as a hard-driving vocalist, composer, and guitarist with the 1975 album "Born To Run" and No. 1 albums in the 1980s, including "The River" and "Born In The U.S.A." His chart-topping success (including many singles) has continued into the new millennium, especially with The E Street Band. (AP Photo via EMPICS)

Status Quo

Status Quo
performing in
Oxfordshire, England,
as part of the BBC
Children in Need
Appeal, November 18,
2005. The band
originated as The
Scorpions formed by
Alan Lancaster and
Francis Rossi in 1962,
then The Spectres and,
with personnel
changes (including
recruitment of Rick
Parfitt), became Status
Quo in 1967. The
high-energy, heavy
beat, head-banging
band has enjoyed huge
popularity in Europe,
particularly in the UK,
with such singles as
"Down, Down,"
"Rockin' All Over The
World," and "In The
Army Now," but never
really made it in the
U.S. charts.

Steely Dan

Leaders of the 12-piece jazz-rock band Steely Dan, Donald Fagen (on keyboard in the spotlight) and Walter Becker (on guitar, far left), at the International Forum Hall in Tokyo, May 2000. The band was formed in 1972 and toured extensively, while its debut album "Can't Buy A Thrill" spawned the high-charting single "Do It Again." Another massive hit was the 1974 "Rikki Don't Lose That Number." The band chose to be a studio-only recording outfit, releasing the acclaimed and successful album "Aja" in 1977, then disbanded in 1981, but Fagen and Becker, having gone solo, surprisingly reformed it and released its first album in twenty years, the Grammy Award-winning "Two Against Nature," in 2000. (AP Photo via EMPICS)

Cat Stevens

Yusuf Islam, the controversial British singer/songwriter formerly known as Cat Stevens, performs during a fund-raising concert for the victims of the 2004 Asian tsunami in Jakarta, Indonesia, January 31, 2005. In the 1960s and 1970s, Stevens was, first, a folk-influenced pop artist, then folk-rock album star. His chart hits included "Morning Has Broken" and "Another Saturday Night." (AP Photo via EMPICS)

Rod Stewart

British rock star Rod Stewart sings on the open air stage of the Kis Stadium in Budapest, Hungary, June 17, 2005. Born in London in 1945, Stewart has had a fantastic, forty-years-plus career as a band member (including Jeff Beck Group and The Faces) and more particularly as a solo artist whose classic international hits have included "Maggie May," "Tonight's The Night," and "Do Ya Think I'm Sexy?" He is now achieving chart-topping success as a crooner with the "Great American Songbook" series of albums. (AP Photo via EMPICS)

Sting

British singer/songwriter, guitarist, producer, and actor Sting performs at London's Live 8 concert, July 2005. Born Gordon Matthew Sumner in 1951, former frontman for the band The Police, Sting has had a solo career that has been a balancing act between successful music star and active environmentalist. His albums have included "The Dream Of The Blue Turtles" (1985), "Soul Cages" (1991), and "Sacred Love" (2003).

Donna Summer

Disco queen Donna Summer (born in Massachusetts in 1948) had a string of critically acclaimed and chart-topping album releases (including "Live And More" and "Bad Girls") in the 1970s, and her career, which has been bolstered by literally scores of singles, continues to the present day, with No. 1s in U.S. Dance charts as recently as 2005.

Talking Heads

Members of the new wave group Talking Heads (from left, David Byrne, Tina Weymouth, Jerry Harrison, and Chris Frantz) speak to reporters after being inducted into the Rock and Roll Hall of Fame, March 19, 2002, in New York. The band was formed in 1976 and had its heyday in the 1980s, but announced Byrne's departure in 1991; one-off reunions did occur, but the band disbanded with members doing their own things for the rest of the decade. (AP Photo via EMPICS)

10cc

Founder members of 1970s British pop group 10cc, Eric Stewart (left) and Graham Gouldman, during the launch in London, February 1995, of a new recording of the group's 1975 No. 1 hit "I'm Not In Love." It didn't fare anywhere near as well the first version. Two other members, Kevin Godley and Lol Crème, left in 1976 to form a duo, but the band played on (with replacements), scoring particularly with "Dreadlock Holiday."

Thin Lizzy

Lead singer with British rock band Thin Lizzy, Dublin-born Phil Lynott, in London, January 18, 1983, to announce the band's disbandment. After ten years and a string of gold and platinum records, including the hit single "The Boys Are Back In Town," the group called it a day with a marathon tour. Lynott died in January 1986 as a result of an indulgent lifestyle.

Justin Timberlake

Pop superstar Justin Timberlake (born 1981) performs at the Oakland Arena, California, June 6, 2003, during a tour with Christina Aguilera. Formerly frontman for *NSYNC, Timberlake has become hugely successful as a solo performer, his 2002 debut album "Justified" reaching No. 2 in the U.S. and top spot in the UK. (AP Photo via EMPICS)

Tina Turner

One of rock's most gifted vocalists, Tina Turner performs at London's Wembley Stadium in her last ever live performance in the UK, July 16, 2000. Following the 1976 split from husband and duo-partner Ike (a relationship that had already revealed Tina's prodigious talents with songs such as "Nutbush City Limits" and "River Deep – Mountain High") she employed rock/R&B/pop/styles to outperform on stage and in recordings pretty well every other female star, with unforgettable tracks such as "What's Love Got To Do With It?," "Private Dancer," and "The Best." While she has given up touring, she has made one-off recordings and many live TV appearances.

U2

Supergroup U2's The Edge and Bono perform at TD BankNorth Garden in Boston, December 4, 2005. The Irish award-winning rock band has been enormously successful for twenty years, with six chart-topping albums in the U.S. alone. Bono in particular has been a tireless supporter of charities involved with world poverty and environmental issues, and it is surprising that he and the band find time to tour and record, so fans will be overjoyed to hear that further releases are planned. (AP Photo via EMPICS)

Van Halen

Van Halen heavy metal guitarist Eddie Van Halen in performance, August 5, 2004. The band has been a major influence on others of the same genre and one of the highest selling of all time. During a twenty-year period from 1978 the band released eleven high-charting albums (with various lead singers). Nothing new was forthcoming from the band between 2000 and 2004, but fans were anxiously waiting for developments in 2005-2006 following rumors that the band was to burst into action again. (AP Photo via EMPICS)

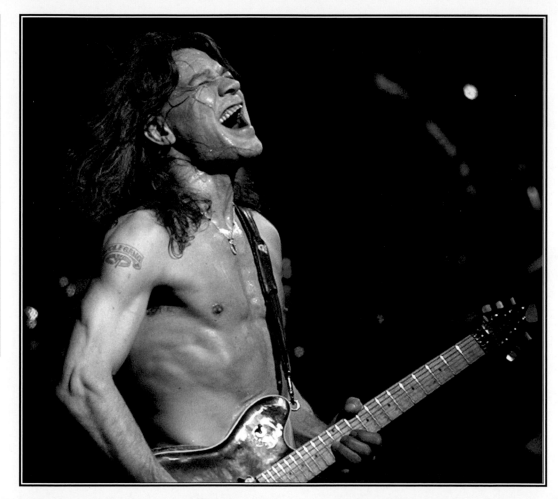

The Walker Brothers

The Walker Brothers (actually unrelated)—left to right, John Maus, Gary Leeds, and Scott Engel—in London in 1967 at the start of a pop tour. Formed in 1964, the Californian group found fame and fortune in the UK rather than their homeland, with "The Sun Ain't Gonna Shine Anymore" and "Make It Easy On Yourself," among others, before splitting in 1967 and then reforming for the one-off, "No Regrets," almost a decade later.

The Waterboys

Mike Scott from the British folk rock band The Waterboys performing during the Fleadh 2001 Music Festival in London. The band was formed in 1983, split ten years later, then reformed in 2000 to tour and release albums. Earning some chart successes in the UK, it is waiting for its appearance in the U.S. charts.

Dionne Warwick

Highly successful singer Dionne Warwick performs her last ever London date, September 3, 2005, as part of her farewell tour following a forty-year career full of high-charting singles (such as "Walk On By," "I Say A Little Prayer," and "That's What Friends Are For"—with Gladys Knight, Stevie Wonder, and Elton John), as well as albums.

The White Stripes

Detroit rock/country/blues band The White Stripes—Jack (vocals, guitar) and Meg (vocals, drums) White—in London, November 9, 2005. The duo broke into the charts with the album "White Blood Cells" in 2001 and have gone on to further commercial success with "Elephant" in 2003 and "Get Behind Me Satan" in 2005.

The Who

Roger Daltrey, left, lead singer, and Pete Townsend, on guitar, of the explosively creative British rock group The Who, perform "Tommy" at Radio City Music Hall in New York, June 27, 1989. Becoming known for gig-ending instrument-trashing sessions, but also for prodigious talent in live and recording performances, the band had its heyday in the late 1960s and 1970s, progressed through various splits, reunions, and personnel changes in the 1980s, continued to perform sporadically in the 1990s, played at the Live 8 concert in 2005, and has left fans hoping for a much-anticipated international tour. (AP Photo via EMPICS)

Robbie Williams

British superstar pop singer Robbie Williams performs in Germany, December 10, 2005. Born in 1974, and formerly a member of the successful boy band Take That, Williams launched a solo career in 1995 and has battled through drink and drugs problems to achieve massive international commercial and critical recognition, his award-winning 1997 single "Angels" being lauded as the best song for twenty-five years. While he has regularly hit the UK No. 1 spot with albums and singles, after ten years as a solo performer he has failed so far to climb high in the U.S. charts. (AP Photo via EMPICS)

Wings

Wings band with Paul McCartney in concert in London, October 19, 1976. Following the breakup of The Beatles, McCartney formed Wings with his then-wife Linda, drummer Denny Seiwell, and singer/guitarist Denny Laine in 1971. For the next ten years the band (with various lineup changes) performed and recorded successfully, highlighting with the 1973 album "Band On The Run" and the 1977 single "Mull Of Kintyre," before disbanding in 1981.

Stevie Wonder

Stevie Wonder, right, receives a hug from Kid Rock following their performance at the World Music Awards in Los Angeles on August 31, 2005. The enormously talented vocalist, multi-instrumentalist, composer, and producer Wonder, a former Motown star, has notched up eleven chart-topping singles and thirty-plus album hits that have had a major influence on R&B and pop music in a career spanning over forty years. (AP Photo via EMPICS)

Wu-Tang Clan

The New York hip hop group Wu-Tang Clan performs at the BET Harlem Block Party, September 10, 2000. The band was formed in 1992 with nine members in the lineup (reduced to eight on the death in 2004 of one of the founder-members, Ol' Dirty Bastard), and achieved success with, in particular, "36 Chambers," while (as had been planned from the start) individual members pursued side projects, getting back together for tours in 2005-2006. (AP Photo via EMPICS)

Yes

The British progressive rock band Yes (left-right, Jon Anderson, Alan White, Chris Squire, Steve Howe and Rick Wakeman) during an in-store signing for its new DVD 'Yes Acoustic', at HMV Oxford Street, London, June 17, 2004. The band had its heyday in the 1970s with internationally high-charting albums such as "Fragile" (1971) and "Close To The Edge" (1972), and singles (including the No. 1 "Owner Of A Lonely Heart") before splitting up and re-uniting a few times, with fans hoping for further album releases in 2006-2007.

Neil Young

Canadian singer/songwriter and guitarist Neil Young performing during the Fleadh 2001 Music Festival in London. Born in Ontario in 1945, Young has been a member of the Buffalo Springfield (1960s) and Crosby, Stills, Nash & Young (1970s) bands and has succeeded in an influential and experimental solo career, while being outspoken and active over conservation issues.

Frank Zappa

Born in Maryland in 1940, the highly talented musician, composer, vocalist, and guitarist Frank Zappa died December 4, 1993. The controversial, politically active Zappa's legacy includes more than sixty albums, many of which achieved commercial success and critical acclaim, highlighted by high-charting "Apostrophe" in 1974. (AP Photo via EMPICS)

ZZ Top

The country/blues, delta, hard rock band ZZ Top performs at its induction into the Rock and Roll Hall of Fame, March 2004, in New York. The band hit the big time with the album "Tres Hombres" in 1973, and ten years later with "Eliminator." Singles success had been enjoyed with the likes of "Tush" (1974), and then "Legs" (1984) and "Sleeping Bag" (1985). Fans anticipate a further album of new material.